Clear Toy Candy

Clear Toy

Candy

All About the Traditional Holiday Treat with Steps for Making Your Own Candy

NANCY FASOLT

STACKPOLE
BOOKS

To the late Cecelia Malone of Celie's Sweet Shop,
the sweet lady who taught me to make clear toy candy

and

My wonderful husband, the late Terry Fasolt,
without whose support, research assistance, and
computer expertise this book would still be a dream

Copyright © 2010 by Stackpole Books

Published by
STACKPOLE BOOKS
5067 Ritter Road
Mechanicsburg, PA 17055
www.stackpolebooks.com

Printed in China

10 9 8 7 6 5 4 3 2 1

FIRST EDITION

Photography by Allen Holm unless otherwise noted
Title page photo by Nancy Fasolt
Cover design by Tessa J. Sweigert

Library of Congress Cataloging-in-Publication Data

Fasolt, Nancy.
    Clear toy candy : all about the traditional holiday treat with steps for making your own candy / Nancy Fasolt. — 1st ed.
       p.   cm.
    Includes bibliographical references.
    ISBN-13: 978-0-8117-3610-7 (pbk.)
    ISBN-10: 0-8117-3610-5 (pbk.)
    1. Candy. 2. Holiday cookery. 3. Toys in art. I. Title.
TX791.F38   2010
641.8'53—dc22

                                           2010002188

Contents

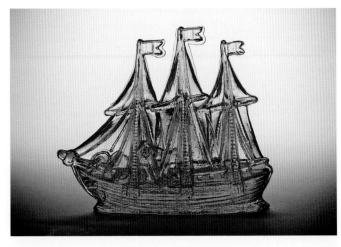

Introduction

G rowing up on the outskirts of Pennsylvania Dutch Country, I have known clear toy candy for as long as I can remember. It was the candy our family looked forward to every Christmas.

In adulthood, I began making cakes and candies and opened a business, the Cake And Kandy Emporium, to sell my goods. One of my first employees had a small grocery store, and before Christmas one year, she invited me to visit. I was speechless when she opened a large red, white, and green can labeled Shellys Candy Toys. The entire twenty-pound can was filled with the colorful clear toy candy I so fondly remembered from my childhood. Shortly after that, Shellys was sold and the new owner discontinued the production of clear toy candy. At that point, as a candymaker, I felt obligated to begin making clear toy candy and keep the tradition alive.

Meanwhile, the Cake And Kandy Emporium became a haven for cake decorators and candymakers. I attended all available shows and brought highly qualified instructors from the United States and Canada into my shop to teach classes. Clear toy, however, became the trademark of the business. In keeping with my mission of preventing the disappearance of the clear toy candy tradition, I produced a clear toy candy kit, so it can be once again produced in the family kitchen. Today I am working through my Web site www.cleartoycandymoulds.com.

The intent of this book is to provide more information on making this crystal-clear candy toy, so that it may be enjoyed by future generations. By offering a study of the molds, ingredients, recipes, and the methods of both today and yesteryear, I hope to encourage you to keep clear toy candy as a cherished Christmas tradition.

Facing page: Nancy Fasolt, left, making clear toy with her daughter Carrie.
JOHN HERR

Yesterday and Today

Clear toy candy is essentially hard, crystal-clear, edible shapes made from a solution of sugar, water, corn syrup, and food coloring. The shapes are formed when the hot solution is poured into molds in which the candy quickly hardens. Barley sugar candy can also be found on the market. Clear toy and barley sugar candy do have a slight difference in taste. In barley sugar candy, barley water is added to the concoction, while clear toy is made from pure water. Both candies are poured into the same molds and are made with or without sticks.

Crystal sugar candy was known in medieval Persia. In medieval Europe it was a luxury, and clear sugar figurines were distributed at the end of banquets. For common folk, the figures became associated with Christmas because of their festive qualities. Clear toy candy became popular in Germany, and barley sugar candy was favored in the British Isles. As the cultures of the British and German settlers began to blend in the United States, however, so did their candy traditions.

In Scotland, the treat was called barley candy or barley sweets, while in England it went by the name barley sugar. Originally, barley sugar was cut into strips and twisted. In the seventeenth century, the twisted sticks were made by boiling down sugar with barley water and cream of tartar.

Facing page: Clear toy candy advertisement, circa 1900.

In the following century, the solution was cast into metal molds in the forms of birds, animals, and other shapes. When this process became common, barley sugar became known as barley toys or barley sugar toys. In recent years, the cream of tartar has been replaced by corn syrup, which increases the candy's durability.

Traditionally in the United States, the colors used for clear toy were yellow, red, and green. Yellow is the natural color of the syrup, so no food coloring was necessary for yellow toys. The red toys were made by adding

Dorothy Timberlake began making barley candy in 1971 in Madison, New Hampshire, and developed a business that lasted until 2009. Pictured here in the 1980s, Dorothy prepares barley candy lollipops.
DOROTHY TIMBERLAKE CANDIES

Above: "Clear Toys" manufactured by Robertson's Candy, Truro, Nova Scotia.
NANCY FASOLT

red coloring to the syrup. Green coloring came from a mixture of yellow and blue colorings. Today, some manufacturers have put their own twist on the candy by offering a variety of colors and flavors. Before its recent closing, Dorothy Timberlake Candies of Madison, New Hampshire, for instance, specialized in dozens of flavors of barley candy, including banana, passion fruit, wintergreen, coffee, horehound, clove, and even jalapeno.

In Germany, clear toy candy continues to be an Easter tradition. It is called *roter zuckerhase*, which translates as the red sugar hare. The sugar hare is the hollow form of clear toy candy, made of sugar boiled in water, corn syrup, and red coloring.

In Canada, Robertson's Candy of Truro, Nova Scotia, produces between thirteen and eighteen tons of clear toy candy or barley sugar candy each Christmas season. When they label it "clear toy candy," they receive letters from customers who want barley sugar candy. When they label it "barley sugar candy," they hear from those who want clear toy candy. Regardless of the label, however, the candy sells about the same.

William Daw Startup began one of the first candy companies that produced and sold clear toy candy. STARTUP CANDY

Clear Toy Candymakers

One of the oldest companies in the United States selling clear toy candy is Startup Candy of Provo, Utah. William Daw Startup came to the United States from England in the 1860s. His father was a confectioner in Manchester who had developed a hard candy medicine he called American Cough Candy.

Startup left England with his father's recipes and candy tools. When he arrived in Philadelphia, he purchased other equipment, including clear toy candy molds. He then traveled by ox caravan to Utah, where in 1874 he established a candy store in Provo near the Brigham Young Academy. In addition to other confections, he made mostly hard candy animals, using the molds he brought with him. Today, the company makes traditional chocolates, drops, pops, licorice, and during the Christmas season, scores of magnificent clear toy candy in a variety of figures, from horses to Santas.

Regennas Candy is another family business that specializes in clear toy. C. Fred Regennas began selling his confections from a horse-drawn wagon in Philadelphia in 1894. Later, he returned to his native town of

Lititz, Pennsylvania, where the tradition has been passed down through several generations. The company was run for many years by Charles H. Regennas and his wife Betty. With Charlie's passing, his son Jake is carrying on the clear toy candy tradition.

Another company that made and sold clear toy for years was Young's Candies of Philadel-

C. Fred Regennas and his delivery wagon, Philadelphia, circa 1906. JOHN REGENNAS COLLECTION

Charles Regennas making clear toys in the 1990s. VIRGINIA LAFOND COLLECTION

phia. In 1880, Johan Jung and his family arrived there from Stuttgart, Germany. Shortly after, Johan changed his name to John Young and opened an ice cream and candy stand in Woodside Amusement Park, on the west side of the Schuylkill River, near the Strawberry Mansion. Then in 1897, John designed and opened Young's Candies at 2809 Girard Avenue, in the Brewerytown/Fairmont section of the city. Young's made all their clear toy candy in the colors of red and yellow. The business was passed down through the family and was operated by Harry Young Jr. starting in the 1940s. Harry once explained to me why antique clear toy molds are so

Harry Young Jr. of Young's Candies in Philadelphia carried on the family tradition for many years. VALERIE SMITH COLLECTION

difficult to find. During World War II, he said, Philadelphia had numerous confectioners, and the majority of them sacrificed the molds. They were "thrown into the streets and onto the piles of metal donated to the war effort." When Harry Jr. passed away in 2007, the store was closed and

Ryan Berley operates the Franklin Fountain in Philadelphia. He uses antique molds from Young's Candies to create clear toy for the holidays.
THE FRANKLIN FOUNTAIN

its contents were sold at auction. Ryan and Eric Berley, proprietors of the Franklin Fountain of Philadelphia, purchased the majority of Harry's clear toy molds and now use them to produce candy for the Christmas holiday season.

At its height, Maggie Wolfgang's store at 1013 North George Street in York, Pennsylvania, used four thousand molds, eight tables, nine stoves, and eight persons pouring to make clear toy candy. Her business opened in 1918, and it flourished. Most of Maggie's molds were iron, produced by a local foundry, using her original patterns. Unfortunately, a fire destroyed her building and business.

Maggie Wolfgang and her workers, York, Pennsylvania, circa 1920.
DUDREAR COLLECTION

In the mid-twentieth century, Shelly Brothers of Souderton, Pennsylvania, became the major producer and shipper of clear toy candy in the United States. When the red, white, and green, twenty-pound cans marked "Crystal Clear Toys" arrived in the stores, everyone knew the Christmas season had begun. Shellys designed their own machinery to mass-produce clear toy candy and obtained twenty-eight patents for the devices. The clear toy was stored in humidity-controlled rooms and shipped as far as New Orleans and Chicago. In 1990, however, the company was sold to Brach's of Tennessee, which discontinued the production of clear toy.

Albert Dudrear of York, Pennsylvania, learned to make clear toy candy at the age of ten by watching his cousin. He began collecting clear toy candy molds, eventually amassing an extensive collection. With the assistance of his three children, he began selling his clear toy and earned enough to put all his children through college. For many years the Dudrear family made clear toy candy in July's sweltering heat at the Kutztown, Pennsylvania, Dutch Folk Festival, as well as at several other events.

Shellys' distinctive can in Christmas colors, circa 1980. NANCY FASOLT

Albert Dudrear Jr. making clear toy candy in York, Pennsylvania, 1988.
CHARLES BLAHUSCH

With his molds collection and extensive knowledge of the subject, Dudrear began writing a book about his passion, but passed away before he could complete it. Al's son-in-law, Donald Culp, operating under the name Original Clear Toy Candy, continues the candy-making tradition.

In addition to my own clear toy business through Cake And Kandy Emporium, my student Dan Pongonis, now of Sweets for Sweeties in Paradise, Pennsylvania, has been making and selling clear toy candy for about twenty years.

Clear Toy Candy Traditions

Many people recall fond memories of clear toy candy and the tradition of receiving it on the holidays.

Elizabeth Stitzinger, who grew up in Dietzinen by Stuttgart, Germany, related her childhood memories of Easter when she was in her nineties:

Mother would go out into the forest and gather moss to make nests for me and my sister; then she would hide them in the woods for us to find. On Easter morning, we would go out into the woods to find our nests. How happy we were when we found our nests with two or three small pieces of clear toy candy gently tucked in each nest. They would be rabbits and lambs. We did receive clear toy for Easter and Christmas.

From the 1800s to the mid-1900s, Pennsylvania Dutch children would "set their plates" on Christmas Eve. Each child set their plate on the table where they took their meals. During the night, Christ-Kindle, also known as *Grisch-Kindel*, or Christ Child, brought gifts for good boys and girls and put them on their plates. Gifts received would be nuts, an apple or an orange, and clear toy candy.

Some families believed that Christ-Kindel came through the keyhole on Christmas Eve. Others believed that Christ-Kindel rode through the streets on a donkey. Some families placed a hat, a box, or a basket on the doorstep or on the windowsill filled with hay for Christ-Kindel's donkey. The donkey would eat the hay and Christ-Kindel would leave gifts for the children.

Families with many children would place only one large platter on the middle of the kitchen table on Christmas Eve. On Christmas morning they would divide the nuts, fruit, and clear candy toys that Christ-Kindel brought for them.

A small fresh cedar tree, cut from the fence row, was a typical Christmas tree. Most of the trees were decorated with ornaments made in the home by the family. Garlands of cranberries, popcorn, snitz (dried apples), paper chains, pretzels, peanuts, cookies, and clear toy candy were commonly used as tree decorations. Candles provided light on the trees, turning the clear toy candy into glistening crystals, according to Nancy Roan of the Goschenhoppen Historians.

Clear toy candy demonstrations at the Goschenhoppen Folk Festival in the Perkiomen Valley of Pennsylvania brought back fond childhood memories of church for one participant:

Each child was given a gift of clear toy candy in a little box. We only licked and sucked our clear toys, and then we would wash up our clear toy candy and line them up around the sink to dry. Then we would fight for our own piece. There were too many brothers and sisters and everyone was after the big ones.

On Christmas Eve, Pennsylvania Dutch children set their plates out for Christ-Kindle, who left them fruit, nuts, and clear toys. NANCY FASOLT

From the late 1700s into the early twentieth century, on the last day of school prior to Christmas holiday, Pennsylvania Dutch children in the one-room schoolhouses played a trick on the schoolmaster. It became a tradition that the older boy students would lock the schoolmaster out of the school. These students would arrive early to prepare. Sometimes they would move the desks around to barricade the door. When the school-master arrived, he was not allowed in unless he gave them a treat, usually cookies or clear toy candy.

The following holiday memory comes from a lady who grew up in an orphanage. She describes the orphans' gifts:

At Christmas time, the adults at the orphanage would clear the large table and . . . set up a train track that would go the whole way around the table. They put a Christmas tree in the middle of the table and the train would run all the way around the table . . . It was so much fun to watch. On Christmas day, the train had a very special car to pull around the track. The special car was filled with clear toy candy and each time the train went around the track, one child was permitted to choose one piece of clear toy candy for their Christmas gift. It made us so happy.

Speaking to candy historian Albert Dudrear, an elderly lady summed up the memories of many children during the Depression. "We were very poor during the Depression, but my parents bought each of us four children a clear toy, which we all treasured. We each chose what we would like. For me, it was the train engine 'cause my father worked on the railroad."

Clear Toy Molds

and Their Makers

To start making clear toy candy, you will need to acquire some molds. Antique molds still exist and can be bought from dealers and at public auctions. There are also companies that make new molds, as well as reproduction molds of antique designs. This chapter will provide you with some background on the early mold makers, examples of their designs, and advice on the types that will be best suited for making clear toy candy in the home kitchen.

For many years, most clear toy molds were made of either iron or an alloy of tin and zinc called "composition." Composition molds were the best quality, because they pulled the heat out of the syrup and cooled quickly.

Beware of molds made of lead or pewter. The lead molds are easily identified, because they look and feel like a sinker used in fishing. Lead and pewter molds should not be used for food production; they are harmful to the human body. When in doubt, take your candy molds to a metallurgy facility and have them tested.

When coming across an old clear toy candy mold, don't be afraid to get your hands dirty. Check the overall condition of the mold. Rust and dirt can sometimes be removed easily.

Molds come in two parts. Put them together to check for tightness. If the sides are not meshing properly, it is possible you will have leakage. Remember that the mold will be cold when the syrup is poured; therefore, depending on the width of the separation, the syrup will set quickly with a bit of flashing on the sides. Flashing is excess candy that forms on the edges of the toy from leakage. You can later trim or file the flashing for smooth edges on your clear toy.

Look for the manufacturer's mark on the mold. Match the marks on both halves to be sure they belong together.

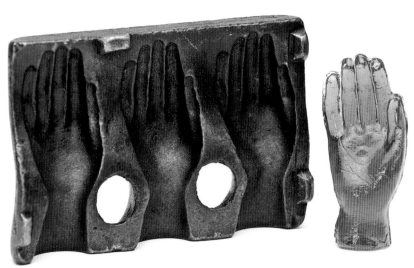

V. Clad & Sons #3 Hand iron mold with manufacturers mark, interior detail, and finished clear toy.

V. Clad & Sons

In the mid-nineteenth century, the port of Philadelphia welcomed many immigrants searching for new opportunities. Among them was Valentine Clad, arriving from the Alsace region of France. He opened his business in 1853, making cooking apparatus and candy and ice cream machinery and tools, including clear toy candy molds. Valentine's sons, Louis and Eugen, joined the business in 1892, and the company was incorporated in 1896 as V. Clad & Sons. The company manufactured its clear toy candy molds in iron.

The V. Clad & Sons catalog displayed scoops, copper pans, cherry stoners, ladles, corkscrews, and furnaces of iron and sheet metal, as well as their own Philadelphia Milk Shake Machine. They also featured a candy toy machine having crank and power capabilities, with rollers containing a total of eighty-six stand-alone patterns. These machines could be purchased by candymakers who wanted to mass-produce clear toys in a quick and efficient way.

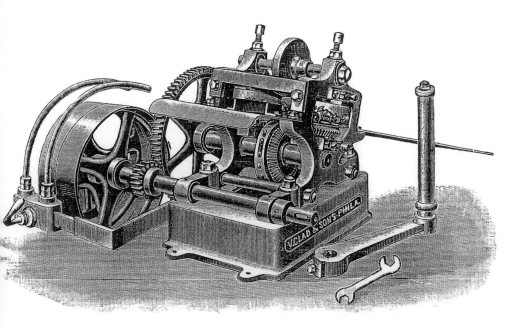

Clear toy candy machine from the V. Clad & Sons catalog, circa 1890.
DUDREAR COLLECTION

Thos. Mills & Bro. factory in Philadelphia. DUDREAR COLLECTION

Thos. Mills & Bro.

The main local competition for V. Clad & Sons was Thos. Mills & Bro. Thomas Mills and his younger brother George arrived in Philadelphia in 1864 from Melrose, Scotland.

Thomas was a skilled machinist, and he and George began the business with $1,000 cash. Working hard long hours and investing wisely, they built a factory by 1893 that occupied an entire city block. Like V. Clad & Sons, they produced clear toy molds and hand-crank and power machinery for the production of clear toy, as well as ice cream freezers, baker's tools, a wide variety of confectionary tools and machinery.

The molds Mills made were produced in the tin and zinc alloy known as composition, which is superior to iron in retaining the distinct detail of the molds. A pattern mold of brass or bronze was made for each mold they manufactured. The pattern mold was used strictly for producing molds, not for making candy.

Unable to keep up with the demand for the clear toy candy molds, Mills reached an agreement with Clad to manufacture some molds for

Thos. Mills & Bro. #194 Giraffe bronze pattern mold.

T. Mills & Bro. mold mark showing date of patent.

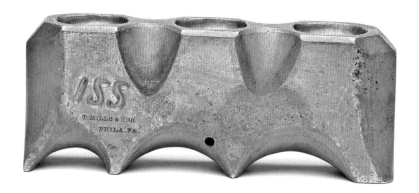

Thos. Mills & Bro. #155 Squirrel composition mold with manufacturer's mark, interior detail, and finished clear toy.

them. Mills, however, required Clad to produce the Mills molds using composition. That is why, as the story goes, it is possible to find molds with a T. Mills & Bro. mark on one half and a V. Clad & Sons mark on the other half of the mold.

The demand for clear toy candy increased substantially at the turn of the century, so Mills designed and sold several machines to mass-produce clear toys, such as the Power Drop Machine, the Universal Sugar Toy Machine, and the Excelsior Clear Toy Machine.

The Mills composition clear toy molds were sold as a set of fifty for $16. Each mold contained one toy with one, two, or three cavities, totaling 125 candy toys if all fifty molds were poured.

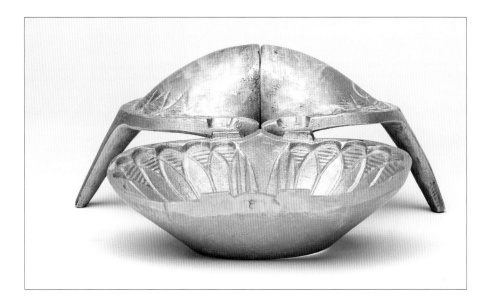

Thos. Mills & Bro. #24 Large Basket composition mold and finished piece of clear toy candy.

Eagle and Sailboat molds from set of fifty molds from Thos. Mills & Bro.

A catalog titled "Pamphlet No.14-F," from the early 1900s offers 285 composition clear toy candy molds, with small patterns containing three, four, five, or six toys in each mold; nineteen three-part molds with three toys per mold; eighteen patent hollow toy molds with one toy per mold; and 103 large patterns of clear sugar toy molds with one, two, three, or four toys per mold.

Copper toy pans were offered at $8 for a 2-quart pan, $10 for a 4-quart pan, and $12 for a 6-quart pan. Aluminum 2-quart toy pans were available for $3.25. Both types displayed sharp spouts for accurate pouring.

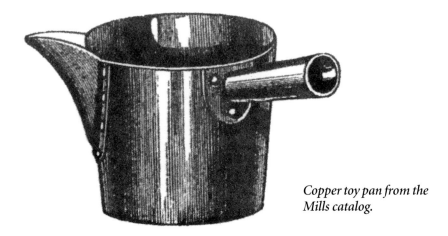

Copper toy pan from the Mills catalog.

Thos. Mills & Bro. #8 Lion composition mold designed by Leonhard Schulze, with its finished clear toy.

Leonhard Schulze, the prominent mold designer for T. Mills & Bro., designed eighteen hollow clear toy candy molds. He received a patent for each one in 1866.

"New Die Cast Clear Toy Moulds, Large Openings, Three Impressions to Each Mould" was the motto of Karl Hohnstock, a dedicated designer for T. Mills & Bro. At Hohnstock's retirement, the Mills brothers gave him many of their master molds. Karl used the master molds to produce molds for several years, but unfortunately, he did not mark his molds. Karl retired in the 1940s and T. Mills & Bro. filed for bankruptcy in 1946. Shortly thereafter, the company was closed.

Other Clear Toy Mold Manufacturers

At the time of the nation's centennial, Thos. J. Andress & Co. of Philadelphia introduced "New Designs of Hollow Toy Moulds, for Making Clear Toy Candy." Some of the new mold designs included the Pope Reading,

Mold mark and interior detail of a Crandell & Godley mold.

Interior detail of molds possibly made by Crandall & Godley with manufacturer's "H" mark. WILLIAM TIMBERLAKE COLLECTION

Opera Dancer, Hippopotamus, Balloon, Padlock, Seal, Bow and Arrow, and 1776–1876 Centennial. Each mold sold for $1.

Crandall & Godley of New York, advertised as importers, manufactures, and jobbers, apparently produced clear toy molds. Crandall & Godley marks appear on a few molds I found in recent years.

Other molds believed to have been manufactured by Crandall & Godley contain no exterior markings and others contain only markings of letters from A to L on the interiors of the molds.

Kiddie Kandie molds depict scenes from the English nursery rhyme "Hey Diddle Diddle," including the Cat and the Fiddle, the Cow Jumped over the Moon, and the Dish Ran Away with the Spoon. A few other Kiddie Kandie molds relate to Easter and Christmas. I have uncovered a few other Kiddie Kandie molds recently: Santa filling his pack (#200), Santa with pack on chimney (#202), chick on egg and chick hatching (#210), two chicks on egg shells (#211), rabbit leaping from egg (#212), and a rabbit standing with paw on sitting rabbit (#213).

Kiddie Kandie #223 The Dish Ran Away with the Spoon mold with manu-facturer's mark, interior detail, and finished clear toy.

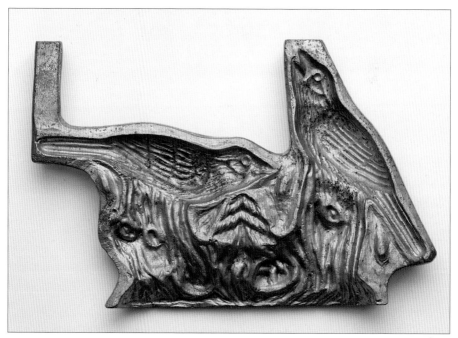

J. Therein mold mark and interior detail.

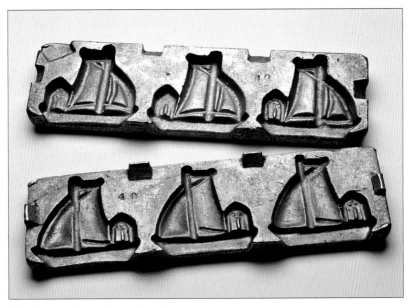

Fletcher mold mark and interior detail.

Clear toy candy or barley sugar candy molds were also manufactured in Canada. Half a mold of beautifully detailed birds marked "J.T. 1946," for J. Therien of Montreal, has been discovered. Fletcher Manufacturing Company of Toronto also manufactured precisely machine-tooled molds.

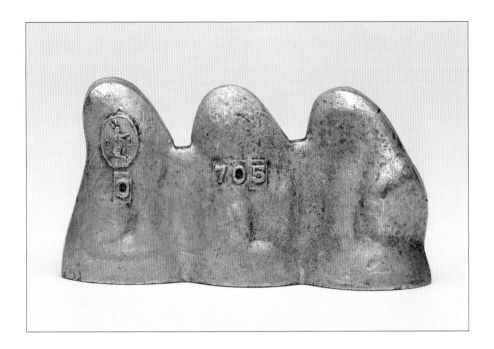

G. Lieb rabbit mold with manufacturer's mark and interior detail.

G. Lieb large rabbit mold and manufacturer's mark.

Easter in Germany sets the scene for *roter zuckerhase* (red sugar hare). The *roter zuckerhase* is made of the same ingredients as clear toy candy in America. The mold, however, is filled with syrup and turned upside down over the kettle, so that the excess syrup is allowed to flow back into the kettle, resulting in a hollow rabbit. The molds were manufactured by G. Lieb in Stuttgart from 1868 to 1960. The Lieb factory produced numerous molds, many of them rabbits with very nice detail and the possibility of three distinct mold markings. One mark is a rabbit sitting up on his hind legs in an ellipse with ears up and elbows flexed. The second mark is a two-letter combination with a G in front of an L. The third mark is the assigned number of the mold.

Clear Toy Molds Today

In the 1990s, the John Wright Company of Wrightsville, Pennsylvania, introduced iron molds with a nonstick coating. No more oily molds. Unfortunately, the entrances to the cavities are quite small and the variances in the depth of the cavities results in quite a bit of candy breakage.

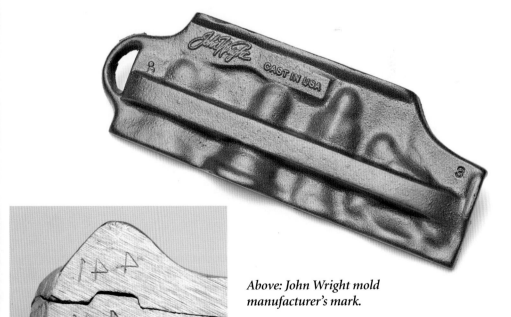

Above: John Wright mold manufacturer's mark.

Left: Cake And Kandy Emporium mold mark.

Cake And Kandy Emporium has reproduced a selection of antique clear toy candy molds from its vast collection. The company will also reproduce your antique clear toy candy molds for you. All molds are hand-produced of food-safe aluminum. The match numbers on their molds are stamped in reverse. Matching numbers are stamped into each half of the mold to identify the matching halves. Their molds have no other markings.

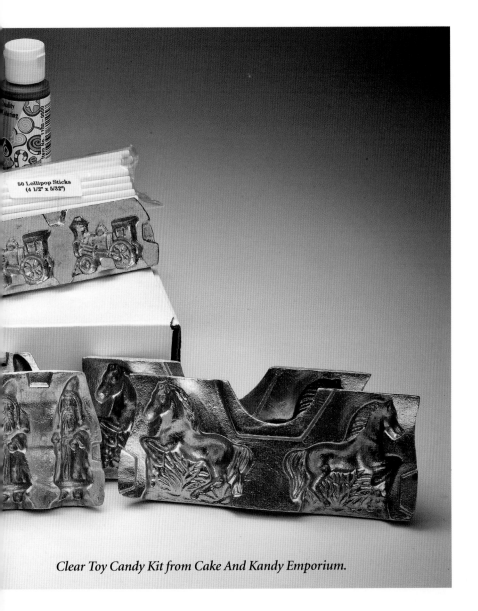

Clear Toy Candy Kit from Cake And Kandy Emporium.

In its effort to continue the tradition of this historic candy, Cake And Kandy Emporium has assembled a clear toy candy-making kit that includes four food-safe aluminum molds (#216 locomotive, #98 horse, #203 basket, and #232 Santa Claus), red and green food coloring, twelve mold closures, fifty lollipop sticks, and fifty cellophane bags, along with its own recipe.

Ingredients

Sugar, corn syrup, water, and red and green food coloring are the only ingredients used in making clear toy candy.

Sugar

Table sugar is mostly derived from sugarcane, although other types are common from corn, sugar beet, sugar maple, palm, date, sorghum, honey, and various fruits. When selecting sugar for clear toy candy, carefully read the ingredients on the sugar package prior to purchase. Often other ingredients are added to cane sugar. Use only packages labeled "pure cane sugar" when making clear toy. The additives will adversely affect your candy.

When sugar is dissolved in water and boiled, it becomes inverted. The inversion is in proportion to the dilution at the time of heating and the natural or process-formed acidity.

Corn Syrup

To complete the inversion of the sugar into syrup for clear toy candy, "doctors" such as vinegar, cream of tartar, or corn syrup are needed. The amount of invert sugar in a confection must be accurate. Candy manufacturers welcomed corn syrup as one of the most practical of all doctors and continue to use it in the making of many confections. Good, crisp hard candy is the result.

Facing page: In nineteenth-century America, families bought sugar in cones wrapped in blue paper. The sugar was snipped from the cone a little at a time by using sugar tongs.

Sugar, corn syrup, and water—the essential ingredients of clear toy candy.

Economical and easy to use, corn syrup in the right proportion coats the sugar molecules with a film to prevent the reforming of crystals. Corn syrup also aids in retention of moisture and freshness in the prolonging of the shelf life of candy. It comes in varying degrees of moisture content. For clear toy candy, 42DE (dextrose equivalent) is recommended. You can make your clear toy with light corn syrup; although it has additives included, resulting in a shorter shelf life, it is preferable to dark corn syrup, which should not be used because of its color. Avoid corn syrup with flavorings.

Water

Throughout history, whatever water was available was used in production of confections. Today, we have access to fresh, clear water. Impure water leads to candy that is discolored and often has an unpleasant odor. Well water needs to be tested by a certified company and municipal water is sometimes cloudy, so be alert. Water obtained from bottling companies and water authorities is typically safe and good to use for clear toy.

Food Coloring

The traditional colors of clear toy candy are red, yellow, and green; however, there are some candymakers who will make only red and yellow candy.

Food coloring is easily found in your local grocery store. You will need only red and green. Yellow is the natural color of the syrup mixture, so you won't need to add coloring for yellow clear toys. According to *The Candy-Maker: A Practical Guide to the Manufacture of the Various Kinds of Plain and Fancy Candy* from 1878,

> It is better for the candy maker to purchase his colors. The colors should be vegetable for it is no doubt true, that mineral colors, merely from being mineral, are harmful, though in some cases not actually poisonous. Aniline is an oily poisonous liquid for making dyes. The colors, though very bright, should be carefully avoided.

Red is the most frequently used color in making clear toy candy. It is derived from cochineal, an insect native to Latin America. Dried pregnant females of the species are used to make the food coloring, which is also called cochineal. Approximately ninety thousand insects are required to produce 2 pounds of cochineal. Green coloring was sometimes produced by adding spinach juice to water. It is typically made from a mixture of yellow and blue colorings. Yellow is made from saffron, a spice obtained from the stigmas of the crocus flower. Blue is produced from indigo, which is derived from a number of plants, particularly those of the genus *Indigofera*.

Professional-quality certified food colorings with a water base produce a brilliant color for your clear toy candy. The red contains water, propylene glycol, red #40 and blue #1. The green coloring contains water, propylene glycol, blue #1 and yellow #5. No coloring is needed for yellow, because the syrup has a natual yellow hue. All the colors will vary, however, depending on the temperature of the syrup and amount of color added. As the temperature exceeds 300 degrees F, the syrup will begin to burn, producing a darker-color candy. Familiar grocery store colorings appear to be slight in color. A great deal of this coloring is needed for bright, crystal-clear results.

Vegetable Oil

Although not really an ingredient of the clear toy, vegetable oil is needed to coat the inside of the molds, so that the candy will not stick when it hardens.

Early candymakers oiled their molds with olive oil. When I began making clear toy candy, I used olive oil to keep with tradition. I found, however, that children would take one lick of the candy, make a strained expression, and tell me they did not like it. I switched to a spray vegetable oil and got a different response. The children loved the candy.

Making Clear

Toy Candy

C lear toy candy is easy to make if the conditions are right. Follow these steps and you will be on your way to making this delicious treat and continuing a favorite holiday tradition.

When to Make Clear Toy Candy

Before you start making clear toy, check the weather report. The temperature must be in the 40s or below, with very low humidity. The colder and drier the weather, the more quickly the clear toy will set, resulting in crystal-clear candy. Warm and humid conditions tend to produce sticky or cloudy clear toy. Even if the candy looks fine when it is removed from the mold, it could later turn sticky or cloudy. Open the doors and the windows, but only with secure screens in place.

What You Need

To start, first gather your molds and utensils. You will need the following items:

- 5 to 7 clear toy candy molds
- 5 to 7 $1/4$-inch rubber bands
- 2-quart kettle
- Spoon
- Pastry brush
- Thermometer
- Mold opener (an oyster shucker or thin-blade screwdriver)
- Paring knife
- Cellophane bags and closures
- Paper lollipop sticks (optional)
- Vegetable oil for spraying molds

Then gather your ingredients:

- Granulated pure cane sugar
- Pure corn syrup (light or 42 DE)
- Red or green water-based food coloring

For your first batch of clear toy, you will be making fifteen to twenty-one pieces of candy. The size of the cavities in the molds you use will cause the yield to vary. Five to seven clear toy molds will work for a 1-pound batch. The size and number of the cavities in each mold will determine the number of molds needed. Be certain that all molds are clean prior to use. They should be scrubbed with hot soapy water and a stiff brush. Metal molds need to be cold and completely dry. They can be chilled in the refrigerator, but must be free of all moisture when you are ready to pour. Watch the dew point. If a glass ketchup bottle sweats when taken from the refrigerator, so will your molds.

Choose a kettle from which you are able to pour a small stream of syrup. You may want to practice pouring with water to get the proper technique. A kettle with a spout similar to the one pictured works very well, but is not necessary.

Making Your First Batch

Prepare the ingredients:
- 2 cups granulated pure cane sugar
- $2/3$ cup pure corn syrup
- $1/2$ cup water
- Red or green water-based food coloring
- Vegetable oil

Coat the insides of the molds with vegetable oil. Oil may be sprayed or brushed onto the interiors of the mold cavities. Spray lightly to avoid puddles. If puddles form, dab the molds to absorb the excess oil.

Close the molds and secure them with strong, 1/4-inch rubber bands. Place the rubber band around the mold from end to end. This enables the bottom of the mold to sit flat and allows easy access for removing the bands later, particularly if lollipop sticks have been inserted into the candy. Larger three-piece molds, such as baskets, need to be secured with two bands wrapped very tight and going around the mold between the cavities. Very large molds require creative methods of banding. Line the molds up close together, so that when you pour the syrup later, you can do it quickly and without waste.

Combine the water and sugar in the kettle. Stir the mixture until the sugar is dissolved.

Add the corn syrup and mix again. Use a clean pastry brush and water to wash any excess syrup from the inside of the kettle above the level of the mixture. It is important to do this, because if any sugar crystals or corn syrup are left on the sides of the kettle, there is a high probability that the entire batch will "turn," which means it will turn back to sugar or crystallize. Don't worry if some of the water gets into the syrup mixture; it will evaporate during cooking.

Carefully put the kettle on the stove and set the heat at medium high. Do not stir. The mixture will reach boiling and the bubbles will subside. At this point, wash the inside of kettle above the mixture level again with the pastry brush and water. Then insert a thermometer.

Let the mixture cook to 265 degrees F and add the coloring. Do not stir. The boiling action will distribute the color. Remember, if you are making yellow candy, you will skip this step, because yellow is the natural color of the syrup.

Let the temperature reach 280 degrees F. If you do not have a clip or hanger for your thermometer, hold it up at this point so that the ball of the thermometer remains in the syrup but off the bottom of the pan. Hold it there until the temperature of the syrup reaches 300 degrees and then quickly remove the kettle from the heat. Let the bubbles subside.

Pour a thin stream of syrup into the oiled molds. Move down the line of molds. Once you have started pouring, do not stop. Every time you tilt the kettle back, you lose part of a toy.

Continue down the line of molds, pouring until they are all filled.

WRONG

If you pour the syrup while it is still boiling, it will bubble out of the mold causing loss of syrup, extra clean-up, extra-hot molds, and possibly burns. The bubbling also may keep the syrup from filling in some of the crevices, resulting in an incomplete toy.

If you want to add lollipop sticks, you will need an assistant to insert them while you are pouring. The assistant must keep a close watch, standing a minimum of three molds behind the pour.

The syrup sets quickly. Expect to wait only three to five minutes. Tap the candy at the mold opening with the blade of your mold opener. If the opener makes a dent in the candy, it is not ready. Let it set a little longer.

WRONG

If you open the mold too early, the candy toy will be soft and mis-shapen.

If you hear a clicking sound, remove the candy from the mold at once. The candy will be warm but not pliable. Remove the candy quickly or it will freeze in the mold. Freezing occurs when the candy has hardened and cooled in the mold. To remove candy that has frozen in the mold, you will need to chip it out or soak it in hot water.

Your candy toys might have some flashing around the edges. To trim the flashing, you will need a sharp paring knife. For safety, apply an adhesive bandage around the upper part of the thumb of the hand in which you will be holding the knife.

Tips for Using Leftover Syrup

If you have leftover syrup, drop various sizes of puddles onto an oiled baking tin and insert lollipop sticks into the puddles, making flat lollipops. After they harden, sand them down (see page 59). Store the lollipops in an air-tight glass container or seal in cellophane bags.

Here are some examples of successfully completed clear toys.

When your candy has cooled, place each piece into a cellophane bag and seal it. Do not use a plastic bag, which will allow moisture to enter and make the candy sticky and cloudy. Store the candy in a cool, dry environment.

Sanding

In the days before cellophane and wax paper, candymakers "sanded" their hard candy. Sanding is coating the candy with confectioner's sugar. The coating seals the air off, keeping the candy fresh and not sticky.

To sand your candy, let it cool completely and then place it over a steaming pot of water for a moment to make it sticky. Immediately toss the candy into a dish of powdered sugar, covering the entire piece. Then brush off the excess sugar. If you have a lot of small bite-sized pieces, put them all together in a strainer over boiling water, toss the candy into the powdered sugar, and brush off the excess. Store the candy in an airtight glass jar.

Cleaning Up

Clean the kettle between each batch of clear toy candy you make. As soon as all syrup has been poured, begin soaking the interior of the kettle by filling it with hot water and scrubbing it with a thick dedicated dish cloth. Do not put the kettle on the stove again until it is completely free of syrup. A fire could result. If you are making a large amount of clear toy candy, alternate between two kettles. Soak one while the other cooks.

When putting the molds away after the cold season, they need to be scrubbed again. Otherwise, the oil will most likely turn rancid. Use hot soapy water with a stiff brush. Remember, whatever you use to clean the molds must be food-safe.

Making Clear Toy Christmas Tree Ornaments

To make clear toy ornaments, you will need to use cotton string, which is digestible in case of accidental swallowing. Tie the ends together with a knot, making a loop. Position the knot inside the mold at the top, leaving enough of the loop end extending out the other side. Close the mold with the string in place and secure with rubber bands. After following the procedure for making clear toy, you will have an ornament to hang on the tree.

Recipe

Variations

A s you will notice, there are variations in clear toy candy recipes. Some recipes call for vinegar, lemon juice, or cream of tartar. These ingredients are acidic and do the same job as corn syrup: reformatting the sugar crystals, resulting in the natural breakdown, or inversion, of the sugar crystals into fructose and glucose. Their tastes may vary.

The following clear toy candy recipe from 1818 originally appeared in Pricilla Homespun's *The Universal Receipt Book* (Philadelphia: Isaac Riley) on page 177. It was reprinted in 1990 by William Woys Weaver in his excellent book on holiday treats, *The Christmas Cook: Three Centuries of American Yuletide Sweets.*

CLEAR TOYS

4 cups sugar

1 cup water

1/4 teaspoon cream of tartar

Green, red or yellow food coloring

Lemon extract (optional)

Dissolve the sugar, water, and cream of tartar. Do not stir once the syrup begins to boil. Boil hard to just slightly beyond the hard crack stage (325 degrees F), which should take about 15 minutes. Add coloring and lemon flavor if you choose, stirring quickly two or three times. Pour the syrup into molds that must be wired shut so that they do not accidentally pop open. Do not use rubber bands; they will melt.

The sugar will foam up when poured into the metal molds, so be extremely careful about splattering. Pour slowly, a little at a time, but pour steadily. Should you prefer not to use molds, pour large drops of syrup onto clean metal baking sheets. The drops will harden into medallions. Or as the sugar cools, pull it quickly into shapes like glass animals.

Note: If left too long in the molds, the candy will shatter when you try to remove it. On the other hand, if the sugar is still too warm, the figure will pull or stretch when the mold is opened. There is a critical point when the candy is ready; it varies almost from mold to mold and is knowledge that must be acquired through trial and error. As soon as the candy is removed from the mold, trim off the rough spots with a sharp knife, done very carefully, of course, so that no scars are visible.

Clear toy candy with an orange and nuts, a traditional Christmas treat.
JOHN HERR

In 1930s and '40s, Cecelia Malone was the proprietor of Celie's Sweet Shop at 127 Reservoir Street in Lancaster, Pennsylvania. She was the lady who taught me how to make clear toy candy. Cecelia studied at the Liberty School of Candy Making in Philadelphia and kindly gave me her class book, *The Liberty Complete Candy-Making Course* by Amelia M. Harris, in which the following recipe is found.

BARLEY SUGAR TOYS (CLEAR TOYS)

2 cups sugar

6 oz. corn syrup

1/8 teaspoon cream of tartar

1/2 cup water

1/2 teaspoon acetate of soda (to keep your candies from getting sticky)

1/4 teaspoon oil flavorings, such as lemon, orange, or lime

Place sugar, water, cream of tartar, corn syrup, and acetate of soda in saucepan. Stir the batch until the sugar is dissolved, then add coloring enough to produce desired shade. Place on stove. When crystals form on sides of saucepan, brush them away with a stiff brush, dipped in cold water.

When cooked to 300 degrees F, remove from stove, stir in flavoring very gently, then pour it into oiled molds. To oil molds, take a brush which you have dipped into sweet oil. Place stick in but do not remove from molds until cold.

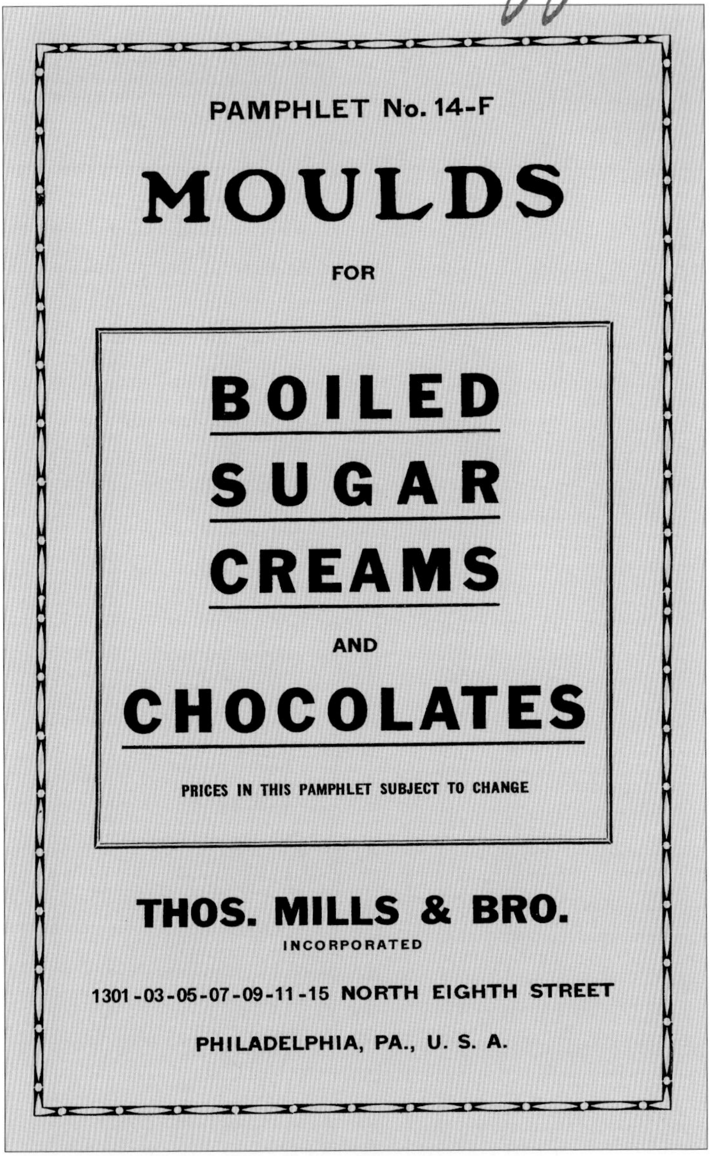

PAMPHLET No. 14-F

MOULDS

FOR

BOILED
SUGAR
CREAMS

AND

CHOCOLATES

PRICES IN THIS PAMPHLET SUBJECT TO CHANGE

THOS. MILLS & BRO.

INCORPORATED

1301 - 03 - 05 - 07 - 09 - 11 - 15 NORTH EIGHTH STREET

PHILADELPHIA, PA., U. S. A.

Thos. Mills & Bro. Molds *From Pamphlet No. 14-F*

COMPOSITION CLEAR TOY MOULDS

SMALL PATTERNS

These Moulds Contain Three, Four, Five and Six Toys in Each Mould

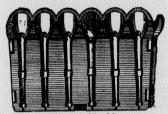

No. 88 Mould

No. 163 Mould

No.	Name	No. in Mould	No. to lb.	Price
1	Horse and Man, large	3	16	$3.50
2	Horse and Man, small	3	48	2.35
3	General on Horse	3	27	2.35
4	Horse	4	45	2.35
5	Horse, small	4	55	2.25
6	Cow	3	38	2.40
7	Sheep	4	30	2.25
8	Dog, large	3	43	2.35
9	Dog, medium	3	48	2.35
10	Dog, small	3	55	2.35
11	Monkey on Horse	3	35	2.35
12	Cat, large	3	28	2.75
13	Cat, small	4	32	2.15
14	Rat	4	32	2.15
15	Deer, small	3	32	2.75
16	Camel	3	45	2.75
17	Rabbit, large	3	16	2.50
18	Rabbit, medium	3	24	2.35
19	Rabbit, small	4	38	2.15
20	Lady on Swan	3	30	2.75
21	Chicken	3	38	2.25
22	Rooster	3	35	2.60
23	Eagle	3	35	2.50
24	Crow	3	40	2.75
25	Bear	4	35	2.35
26	Baby, large	3	32	2.75
27	Baby, small	3	30	2.60
28	Jim Crow	3	64	2.85
29	Man and Wheelbarrow	3	55	2.50
30	Woman and Churn	4	48	2.15
31	Hand	3	38	2.75
32	Basket and Flowers	3	38	2.25
33	Acorn	3	30	2.75
34	Harp	3	32	2.75
35	Fireman	3	24	3.00
36	Tom Thumb	3	48	2.50
37	Soldier	4	48	2.35
38	Steamboat	3	48	2.25
39	Locomotive	3	43	2.25
40	Sloop	3	43	2.25
41	Flat Iron	4	48	2.15
42	Key	3	35	2.75
43	Skate	3	55	2.50
44	Pistol	3	48	2.25
45	Shovel	3	27	2.50
46	Scissors	3	43	2.50
47	Fiddle	4	38	2.35
48	Bugle	3	55	2.50
49	Watch	3	21	2.25
50	Basket with Handle	3	31	2.25
51	Flower Basket with Handle	3	28	2.25
52	Pitcher, small	3	33	2.15
53	Rocking Horse, small	3	35	2.15
54	Three Figures	3	48	2.50
55	Rabbit and Basket	4	16	2.60
56	Locomotive, large	3	14	2.35
57	Church on Hill	3	18	2.35
58	Teapot	3	48	2.75
59	Lion	3	70	2.35
60	Sword	3	27	2.75
61	Boy and Goat	3	43	2.40
62	Watch, small	3	45	2.35
63	Donkey	3	55	2.35
64	Elephant	3	43	2.15
65	Caught in the Act	3	48	2.30
66	Ladders	3	40	2.75
67	Horse and Cart	3	28	2.35
68	Sparrow	3	19	2.60
70	Locomotive, small	3	28	2.30
75	Saucers	3	35	$2.25
81	Gun	4	48	2.50
82	Pistol	4	32	2.85
83	Pocket Knife	4	38	2.40
84	Dirk	4	40	2.60
85	Rooster, small	5	55	2.75
86	Crucifix	3	32	3.00
87	Axe	4	48	2.35
88	Pipe	6	21	4.00
89	Ass	3	25	2.35
90	Deer Lying Down	5	48	2.40
91	Mule	3	21	2.50
92	Dog, large	3	12	3.00
93	Dog with Basket	3	12	3.00
94	Dog Standing Up with Basket	3	15	2.75
95	Peacock	3	21	2.60
96	Decanter	3	19	2.50
97	Boots	5	27	3.00
98	Plain Basket with Handle	3	23	2.50
101	Squirrel and Box	5	33	2.85
102	Broom	3	13	2.85
103	Bust of Napoleon	4	20	3.00
104	Lady's Head	3	28	2.60
105	Cupid	3	21	2.85
106	Rabbit	3	10	3.35
107	Fish on Plate	3	19	2.35
108	Rooster	3	14	2.60
109	Owl	3	16	2.35
110	Cupid with Basket	3	19	2.60
111	Pony	3	18	2.30
112	Dog	3	15	2.50
113	Cat and Dog Fighting	3	18	2.30
114	Grasshopper	3	13	3.25
115	Steamboat	2	19	2.30
116	Sea Lion	3	12	2.35
117	Rhinoceros	3	15	2.30
118	Tiger	3	15	2.30
119	Bear, small	3	20	2.85
120	Bear, medium	3	16	2.25
121	Bear, large	3	8	3.35
122	Ape	3	14	2.25
123	Large Hand	3	11	2.65
124	Bear Sitting Up	3	16	2.35
125	Camel	3	18	2.75
126	Squirrel	3	13	2.50
127	Horse Jumping	3	30	2.50
128	Lamb Lying Down	3	14	2.40
130	Double-pointed Iron	3	16	2.30
131	Boy on Rocking Horse	3	19	2.75
132	Elephant	6	21	2.75
133	Captain Jack	3	18	2.30
134	Frog Smoking	3	16	2.35
135	Swan	3	18	2.25
136	Trumpet	3	16	2.60
137	Boots	3	19	2.30
138	Elephant	3	14	2.15
139	Monkey on Camel	3	20	2.25
140	Cupid on Lion	3	18	2.30
141	Rabbit	4	25	2.25
142	Monkey Dressed in Soldier Clothes	3	25	2.15
144	Sloop	3	12	3.00
145	Rabbit and Wheelbarrow	3	6	3.40
146	Lamb, large	4	14	3.00
147	Monkey on Camel, large	3	8	3.00
148	Boy and Large Lamb	3	11	3.25
149	Pig	3	18	2.25
150	Dog in Kennel	3	15	2.35

COMPOSITION CLEAR TOY MOULDS—Continued

No. 276. Hand

No. 279. Bust of Taft

No.	Name	No. in Mould	No. to lb.	Price
151	Fancy Clock	3	18	$2.35
152	Small Boy	3	30	2.50
153	Mazeppa	3	13	2.75
154	Crane	3	15	2.75
155	Squirrel	3	10	3.00
156	Boy Riding Dog	3	18	2.85
157	Goat Jumping	3	16	2.60
158	Cow with Calf	3	23	2.35
159	Organ Grinder with Monkey	3	24	2.50
160	Kris Kringle, Deer and Sleigh	2	10	2.50
161	Basket	3	19	2.50
162	Baby in Cradle	3	16	2.40
163	Horse	3	20	2.50
164	Soldier Boy	3	13	2.85
165	French Lady	4	15	3.00
166	Fancy Bottles	4	12	2.85
167	Boy Stealing Apples	3	13	3.00
168	Hussar	3	9	3.30
169	Scotchman	3	11	3.30
172	Rabbit Sportsman	3	16	3.00
173	Railroad Car	3	18	2.35
174	Fancy Tea Kettle	3	11	2.85
175	Spread Eagle	2	7	3.00
176	Chinaman and Dog	3	13	2.75
177	Rabbit Traveler	3	16	2.50
178	Frog on Bicycle	3	15	2.60
179	Ostrich	3	12	2.75
180	Tramp	3	12	2.75
181	Fox	2	12	2.35
182	Horse and Jockey	3	19	2.75
183	Piggyback	3	16	2.50
185	Sail Boat	3	15	2.75
186	Irishman and Pig	3	15	2.75
187	Monkey's Piggyback	3	15	2.60
188	Policeman and Boy	3	14	2.75
189	Dog and Deer	3	12	2.85
190	Boy on Bicycle	3	18	2.50
191	Owl in Tree	3	12	2.75
192	Puss in Boots	3	10	3.00
193	Kangaroo	3	11	3.00
194	Giraffe	3	12	3.20
196	Rifle	4	38	2.25
197	Irishman	3	23	2.50
198	Chinaman	3	19	2.35
199	Israelite	3	19	2.35
200	Uncle Sam	3	23	2.25
201	Dutchman	3	16	2.40
202	Dog Sitting Up	3	12	2.75
204	Dog Running	3	21	2.40
205	Shears	3	38	2.60
206	Shovel	3	21	2.60
207	Frog	3	22	2.15
208	Lion	3	22	2.35
209	Tiger	3	22	2.35
210	Cannon	3	20	2.60
211	Turkey	3	20	2.60
212	Small Dagger	3	30	2.25
213	Man in Barrel	3	28	2.35
214	Boy on Bicycle	3	24	2.40
215	Small Hatchet	3	28	2.40
216	Locomotive	3	21	2.40
217	Steamboat	3	21	2.50
218	Baby Carriage	3	17	2.75
219	Canary Bird	3	21	2.60
220	Wolf	3	20	2.60
221	Parrot	3	32	2.50
222	Cat	3	19	2.60
223	Candlestick	3	20	2.85
224	Shepherd Boy and Dog	3	20	2.60
225	Shepherd Girl and Dog	3	20	2.60
226	Fish	3	20	2.85
227	Dolphin	3	20	2.85
228	Tennis Racquet	3	20	2.85
229	Bicycle	3	20	2.50
230	Hen on Nest	3	20	2.50
231	Rabbit Standing	3	20	2.75
232	Santa Claus	4	20	$2.75
233	Man on Horse	3	20	3.00
234	Lady on Horse	3	20	3.00
235	Brownies	3	22	2.75
236	Pipe	4	20	2.75
237	Alligator	2	20	2.25
238	Rat	3	18	2.35
239	Watering Pot	3	22	2.50
240	Lobster	3	20	2.50
241	Punch	3	22	2.75
242	Turtle	3	20	2.35
243	Rooster	3	20	2.75
244	Mary and Lamb	3	18	2.75
245	Boy in Boat	3	18	2.50
246	Puss in Shoe	3	18	3.00
247	Fox and Goose	3	18	2.75
248	Lion with Cubs	3	18	2.75
249	Dog Standing	3	18	3.00
250	Giraffe	3	18	2.75
251	Windmill	3	20	2.50
252	Eagle with Shield and Cannon	3	16	3.00
253	Uncle Sam	3	20	2.75
254	Com. Dewey Bust	3	18	3.00
255	Disappearing Gun	3	18	2.75
256	Battleship	3	16	2.75
257	U. S. Campaign Hat	3	18	3.30
258	Roosevelt Bust	3	18	3.00
259	McKinley Bust	3	18	2.75
260	Owl	3	20	2.25
261	Puss in Shoe	3	25	2.50
262	Sofa	3	22	2.25
263	Duck	3	20	2.50
264	Bear	3	20	2.50
265	Jackass	3	22	2.35
266	Rat and Flour Bag	3	23	2.50
267	Cat and Kittens	3	20	2.35
268	Boy	3	22	2.35
269	Snake on Tree	3	22	2.35
270	Hen and Chicks	3	22	2.25
271	Automobile	4	18	2.50
272	Pipe	4	15	2.75
273	Pipe	4	16	3.00
274	Washington Hatchet	3	20	3.00
275	Eagle Wings Spread	2	16	2.75
276	Hand	5	16	3.35
277	Pipe Bowl	5	16	3.00
278	Bust of Lady	5	16	2.75
279	Bust of Taft	5	14	3.25
280	Hand	5	16	3.00
281	Hand, small	5	40	2.25
282	Possum	5	16	3.25
283	Hand	5	20	3.00
284	Rabbit	5	16	3.20
285	Turkey	4	16	3.25

THREE PART MOULDS

No.	Name	No. in Mould	No. to lb.	Price
69	Small Boat	3	43	$4.00
71	Pitchers	3	31	4.25
72	Sugar Bowl	3	21	4.25
73	Tea Cup	3	40	4.00
74	Coffee Cup	3	21	4.00
76	Tea Pot	3	12	5.00
77	Wine Glass	3	40	4.00
78	Wash Tub	3	33	4.50
79	Flower Vase	3	23	4.35
80	Round Table	3	31	4.25
99	Wine Glass, large	3	18	4.50
100	Fire Horn	3	21	4.50
129	Sugar Bowl	3	21	4.00
143	Pipe	6	33	4.75
170	Rabbit Soldier	3	9	5.00
171	Rabbit Drummer	3	9	5.00
184	Fancy Pitcher, large	3	13	4.50
195	Fancy Pipe	2	13	4.15
203	Basket	3	14	4.50

CLEAR SUGAR TOY MOULDS

LARGE PATTERNS

Represents No. 3 Mould

Represents No. 31 Mould

No.	Name	Size	No. in Mould	Price
1	Deer	5 x7	1	$6.00
2	Deer	3 x7	1	3.75
3	Horse	5½x5½	1	6.00
4	Horse	2½x2½	1	2.50
5	Horse	2½x2½	2	2.75
6	Horse	3 x2½	1	2.50
7	Horse	3 x2½	2	3.00
8	Camel	3 x3	1	2.75
9	Camel	5½x5½	1	6.00
10	Elephant	3 x2	2	4.50
11	Elephant and Boy	3 x3	1	2.75
12	Goat	3 x2¾	2	3.00
13	Cat	5 x4½	1	3.75
14	Cat	3 x4½	1	3.75
15	Dog	6 x4	1	4.50
16	Dog Lying Down	3½x5½	1	3.50
17	Dog	3¼x4¼	2	5.00
18	William Penn	5¼ high	1	2.75
19	Indian	5¼ "	1	2.75
20	Rooster	5 x3½	1	2.75
21	Rooster	3½x3	1	2.15
22	Locomotive	10 x6½	1	18.00
23	Locomotive, Rabbit Engineer	3½x3¾	1	3.25
24	Basket	9 x6	1	12.00
25	Basket	4½x4	1	6.00
26	Priest Blessing Children	2 x6	1	2.75
27	Washington	7 high	1	2.25
28	U. S. Grant, Bust	7½ "	1	3.60
29	Gun	7 long	3	4.50
30	Gun	7 "	1	2.50
31	Ship full sail	7½x6	1	7.00
32	Steamboat	6½x4	1	7.00
33	Row Boat	9 long	1	6.00
34	Row Boat	6 "	1	2.50
35	Row Boat	2½ "	2	3.50
38	Spread Eagle on Half Globe	4 x6	1	8.00
39	Rabbit	5 x5	1	5.00
40	Rabbit	3 x3	2	3.50
41	Lamb	4 x5	1	4.00
42	Lamb	3¼x2½	2	3.00
43	Row Boat	4½x2¼	1	3.50
44	Elephant "Jumbo"	8½x6	1	10.00

No.	Name	Size	No. in Mould	Price
45	Lion	8½x6	1	$10.00
46	Knight on Horseback	3 x5½	1	2.25
47	Fire Engine	5 x7	1	9.00
48	Buffalo	5½x8	1	9.00
49	Ship, full sail	4 x4	1	3.75
50	Pitcher	4 x4	1	6.00
51	Cow	5¼x3¼	1	5.00
52	Kris Kringle	6¼x2⅝	1	5.50
53	Fish	3¾x1½	2	3.50
54	Dolphin	3¾x2	2	3.50
55	Boy Under Grandpa's Hat	3 x1¼	3	3.25
56	Girl with Large Hat	3 x1¼	3	3.25
57	Angel or Baby	6 high	1	4.50
58	Wings for 57		2	2.15
59	Anchor	4 long	2	4.00
60	Columbus	5¾ high	1	3.25
61	Ship, "Santa Maria"	6 long	1	5.00
62	Santa Claus and Chimney	5½ "	1	3.00
63	Santa Claus	4⅜	1	3.00
64	Pug Dog	2¾x3½	1	2.50
65	Pig	2½x5	1	3.50
66	General on Horse	6½x6	1	7.00
67	Boy on Bicycle	6 x6	1	5.00
68	George Washington's Hatchet	4¼x8	1	5.00
69	Eagle, with Shield and Cannon	4 x4¾	1	3.50
70	Uncle Sam	6 x3	1	3.50
71	Com. Dewey Bust	5¾x3¾	1	3.00
72	Disappearing Gun	3⅛x4⅜	1	2.50
73	Battleship	3¾x8¼	1	6.50
74	U. S. Campaign Hat	4¾x4¼	1	3.00
77	Elk Antlers	5 x5	1	3.25
78	Rooster	4½x3	2	4.00
79	Rabbit	4 x2½	2	4.00
80	Pheasant	3⅜x2½	1	2.35
81	Heart	3 x2⅜	2	3.00
83	Automobile	2½x4	1	2.35
84	Running Rabbit	4 x5	1	2.50
85	Horn of Plenty	3½x6	1	4.00
86	Hen	2½x2	2	3.00
87	Santa Claus	4 x1½	3	5.00
88	Automobile	4½x1¾	1	3.50

PATENT HOLLOW TOY MOULDS

No.	Name	Size	Price
1	Fireman	2½x4¾	$3.00
2	Steam Fire Engine	3 x2½	2.50
3	Goddess of Liberty	3¾	2.75
4	Castle	4¾x2½	2.75
5	Elephant	4¼x3	4.00
6	Lighthouse	3	2.35
7	Steamboat	4¼x2¼	2.50
8	Lion	4¼x6	5.50
9	Harvest Field	3 x4	3.00

No.	Name	Size	Price
10	Eagle	2¾	$2.25
11	Dog	3½x2	2.15
12	Bust of Lincoln	4½x2½	2.50
13	Ship in Full Sail	2½x2½	2.00
14	Locomotive	5 x3½	5.00
15	Butterfly	2¼x2¼	2.00
16	Horse	4¾x4½	4.75
17	Anchor	4½x2½	2.50
18	Pennsylvania Coat of Arms	3¾x2½	2.25

Copper Toy Pans

No. 1	2 quarts	$8.00
No. 2	4 quarts	10.00
No. 3	6 quarts	12.00

Wood handles, $0.30

Aluminum Toy Pans

Capacity 2 qts., price $3.25

Sources

Clear Toy Candymakers

Franklin Fountain
116 Market Street
Philadelphia, PA 19106
215-627-1899
www.franklinfountain.com

Cake And Kandy Emporium
717-898-2482
www.cleartoycandymoulds.com

Regennas Candy Shop
717-866-1873
www.clearcandy.com

Robertson's Candy
43 Charles Street
Truro, Nova Scotia B2N 1X2
(902) 895-1708

Startup Candy Company
534 South 100 West
Provo, UT 84601
801-373-8673
www.startupcandy.com

Books and Articles

Harris, Amelia M. *The Liberty Complete Candy-Making Course.* Philadelphia: Amelia Harris Liberty School, n.d.

Meschner, Virginia. "Glossary of Sugar, Syrups, and Other Sweets." *Food History News* 58, no. 2 (Fall 2003): 1–6.

———. "Sugar: From Field to Bowl." *Food History News* 59, no. 3 (Winter 2004): 3–9.

Shoemaker, Alfred L. *Christmas in Pennsylvania.* 50th anniversary ed. Mechanicsburg, PA: Stackpole Books, 2009.

————. *Eastertide in Pennsylvania*. 40th anniversary ed. Mechanicsburg, PA: Stackpole Books, 2000.

Van Arsdale, May G., Day Monroe, and Mary I. Barber. *Our Candy Recipes*. New York: Macmillian, 1929.

Weatherly, Henry. *Treatsie on the Art of Boiling Sugar*. Philadelphia: Henry Carey Baird, 1865.

Weaver, William Woys. *The Christmas Cook: Three Centuries of Yuletide Sweets*. New York: HarperCollins, 1990.

Web sites

Cake and Kandy Emporium. http://cleartoycandymoulds.com

"Clear-Toy Candies." *The Franklin Fountain*. http://franklinfountain philly.blogspot.com/2009/04/clear-toys.html.

"Complete History." *Startup Candy Company*. www.startupcandy.com/CompleteHistory.html.

"History of Clear Toy Candy." *Regennas Candy Shop*. http://www.clear candy.com/history.html.

Acknowledgments

To make this book possible, it took more than a dream. I express gratitude to Harold Guttman, for inviting me to a seminar on how to make hard candy, and the late Cecelia Malone, who came into my newly opened candy store, took several hard looks at my clear toy candy, and declared "someday I am going to teach you how to make clear toy candy." She did.

Many thanks to Eleanor Dudrear, for generously giving me the information her late husband, Albert, had gathered in preparation for writing a book about clear toy candy, and William Timberlake, for giving me a tour of his fantastic collection of candy molds, enlightening me with much-needed clear toy candy history, and being there to answer my questions. Thanks also to my travel buddy, Carol Fournier, for accompanying me on a road trip to visit Dr. Timberlake in New Hampshire and Robertson's Candies in Truro, Nova Scotia, where we met with Blaine Naugler, who devoted many hours to us and provided us with lots of candy for the trip home.

I appreciate the opportunity I was given by editor Kyle Weaver at Stackpole to publish this book and thank him for all his hard work. Thanks also to Sharon Hernes Silverman, who wrote a feature about my clear toy in her book *Pennsylvania Snacks*. She introduced me to Kyle several years ago in Lititz while we were making clear toy candy, leading to this venture.

I thank food historian William Woys Weaver, for meeting with me to discuss Christmas candy and supplying me with a wonderful sugar cone; Melanie Maldonado, for assistance in testing the recipes; Pat Merritt, for coming to Pennsylvania from North Carolina to test recipes and for bringing me an Oster Hare from Germany; my sister, Joan Garner, for her patience and quick response when my computer and I were at odds; and Allan Holm, for the fantastic photographs.

For information on candymakers, mold manufactures, and clear toy tradition, I thank Emily Albert, Harrisburg, Pennsylvania; Ryan and Eric Berley, The Franklin Fountain, Philadelphia; Donald and Lee Culp, York, Pennsylvania; Eleanor Dudrear, York, Pennsylvania; Harold Jenkins, Lansdale, Pennsylvania; Virginia LaFond; Sandra Oliver of *Food History News*, Islesboro, Maine; E. Kenneth Shelly, Lansdale, Pennsylvania; Valerie Smith, daughter of Harry Young; John Startup of Startup Candy Company, Provo, Utah; Faith Timberlake-Alves of Dorothy Timberlake Candies, Madison, New Hampshire; Shirley Wilson, granddaughter of Thomas Mills, for information regarding the family business; the members of Pennsburg United Church of Christ at the Goschenhoppen Festival, for sharing their memories of clear toy candy; and Nancy Roan of the Goschenhoppen Society for sharing info and stories. And many thanks to my family and friends for patience and understanding during the last two years. Now they can stop saying "when is that book going to be finished?"